Contents

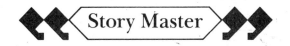

The Bonny

Jo Wilson

Illustrated by Katinka Kew

Edward Arnold

© Jo Wilson 1986

First published in Great Britain 1986
Edward Arnold (Publishers) Ltd
41 Bedford Square, London WC1B 3DQ

Edward Arnold (Australia) Pty Ltd
80 Waverley Road, Caulfield East
Victoria 3145
Australia

British Library Cataloguing in Publication Data
Wilson, Jo
   The Bonny.
   I. Title   II. Woodward, Stephen, *1946–*
   428.6   PR6073.I467/

   ISBN 0-7131-7500-1

Set in 12/14 pt Compugraphic Baskerville by
Colset Private Limited, Singapore.

Printed and bound by Richard Clay (The Chaucer Press) Ltd,
Bungay, Suffolk

Moving In

It was raining. Not pouring down but enough to steam up the car windows. They parked at the back of the house. The van was already there. The men were lifting the old green sofa from the back and the two chairs were in the small yard behind the house. Rob thought it looked like they were going to have a picnic. He rubbed at the window of the car. The stuff was going to get wet. His Mum had been sure it would rain. It had rained last time they moved. That had been before he'd been born.

'Can we have a dog?' he said. He'd really only been thinking about it but there was no harm in asking.

'Let's get moved in Rob,' Mum said, 'the last thing I need to think about today is a dog.' Rob sighed. He hadn't really expected an answer. There never seemed to be a good time to think about a dog.

The removal men were carrying the new rugs which were still wrapped in plastic sheets. The new things in the house would probably be the next reason for not having a pet. Rob sat back in the seat. His Uncle Alex parked the car and Mum leapt out. Dad was already inside helping the men. Rob did not know what to do. He couldn't stay in the car but the house didn't seem ready yet. He could see his bed and his wardrobe still in the back of the big van. He grabbed his sports bag and slammed the car door behind him. He'd put some of his own things that he didn't want to lose into his bag.

He walked through the small yard. They'd had a garden at their old house. His Dad had grown vegetables. There didn't seem to be a vegetable plot here.

His Dad was in the little room behind the kitchen connecting the washing machine to the taps on the wall. Rob sat on the work surface. He pushed his bag underneath.

'What d'you think of it then?' said Dad. Rob shrugged.

'Don't know yet, can't picture it till the stuff is in. It's old isn't it?' Dad nodded.

'Got a bit of character, these houses. Room to stretch.'

'Room for your vegetables?' said Rob. Dad nodded.

'I'll get the back yard organised before the summer. Might even have a greenhouse. We could get some of those seats like they have in the garden centre and some of those tubs.'

'Our other garden was bigger,' said Rob. Dad nodded.

'But this place is ours, Rob. This is what I've wanted, what I've been working for . . . your Mum's over the moon isn't she?' Rob nodded. He

looked out of the little window.

'I'll miss my mates,' he said quietly.

Dad looked up. 'You'll make new mates,' he said. 'I bet when the rain stops there'll be some lads out on that grass behind the back lane . . . there always were when I was your age.'

Rob sighed. It had looked a bit bare. Dad was

still smiling at the memory. 'We called it *The Bonny* because we used to build the bonfire there on the fifth of November. We didn't get cars parked in it then but there was always somebody around. Your Gran's house was the end one at the other side of the lane. I used to be out on that patch by nine o'clock in the morning at the weekend and by ten there was half a dozen of us. We had cricket against Dobson's wall and football in the middle. Your Uncle Alex and I rode our bikes round and round the outside on the cobbles. After the rain there used to be a water splash down the bottom end.'

Rob shifted. If Dad went on any more he'd reach the stage where he talked about how they never needed money 'cause they amused themselves and how he and Uncle Alex were perfectly happy with an old football and a swim in the river in the summer. Rob knew this conversation.

'D'you think Mum will let me have a dog?' he asked. His Dad fixed the rubber tubing to the tap.

'We'll have to think about it Rob,' he said. 'It's a big responsibility. Dogs have to be walked, especially here . . . the main road's so near.' He looked thoughtful.

'Thornbank Hill is just up the road,' Rob said. 'You said you used to go up there all the time . . . it's just grass for miles. I could walk a dog up there.'

Dad nodded. 'It would be good to have a guard dog. It would save me buying one of these expensive alarms. Yes, it's certainly worth thinking about.' Rob hardly dared speak. *That* wasn't a definite no.

'We couldn't have had one at the old house,' Dad continued. 'There just wasn't room and anyway, the place was full of other people's dogs . . . most of them just allowed to run wild. I wouldn't have had that. It's not fair to the animal and they can cause accidents.'

'But it would be different here,' Rob said. 'This is a better place altogether.' He was sure this was what Dad wanted to hear.

'It is that,' said Dad. 'You'll like it as much as I did. It's a great place to grow up. I've wanted to get a place here for ages. It was just a case of waiting till the right house came up and everything was right for a move.'

Rob knew he was talking about work. There'd been a bad time last year when work hadn't been going well and his Dad had been worried about his job. It had passed. Things had worked out but it had been bad at the time.

His mate, Kenny . . . *his* Dad had been made redundant and still didn't have a job. Rob remembered the whispered conversations after he went upstairs at night. He had lain awake listening. Things had worked out though. He looked at his Dad, who seemed really pleased with the house. Even though his Mum was fussing around, he knew she was pleased too.

He thought of Kenny and decided he'd say the

place was great. Leaving his bag tucked under the work surface, he went out into the yard. It had stopped raining. He opened the door of the brick outhouse. There was a pile of old flower pots inside. He closed the door again, walked out of the yard and leaned on the wall. It was quite a big patch of grass with one or two old trees on the edge of it. A fair-haired boy was dragging a plastic dustbin from his yard to the wall. He looked over at Rob. Rob pretended to examine one of the trees. The boy said hello. Rob nodded. The boy walked over towards him.

'You moved into number eight?' he asked.

'Just about,' Rob said, 'though most of our stuff is still in the van. I'm just having a look round.'

'I live in number fifteen,' the boy said. 'If you're out later, I'll see you.'

Rob smiled. 'I was just wondering where the best place to walk a dog is . . . around here?'

'D'you have a dog?' the boy asked.

'Not yet,' Rob said, 'we're thinking about it. I'm sort of . . . making *plans* for one.'

'I'll show you the best places,' the boy said. 'I have to go now but I'll see you later. My name's Daniel . . . see you.'

Rob waved. He walked back towards the yard . . . his yard. His Dad was right. It hadn't taken long and was probably going to be okay. Even better, if Mum would agree to a dog . . . but okay anyway.

10

Skip

Rob cut open a bun and slid the egg from his plate into it. He looked out of the kitchen window. His Mum was watching him. 'Don't suppose I could take this out with me?' he asked. She shook her head.

'You'll eat your breakfast at the table like any normal person. I don't know why we bothered getting a house at all. You seem to spend most of your time outside. Is it Daniel again?' Rob took a bite from his bun and nodded.

'I said I'd meet him early. There's a skip outside one of the houses . . . we want to see what's being flung out.' He looked again out of the window. His Mum sighed.

'I really don't know what it's going to be next and don't bolt your food like that. It's not good for you. Do you want some toast?'

'Haven't time,' Rob said. 'Anyway, this will be fine.'

His Dad laughed at him. 'I remember my Mum used to make bags of chips for us. She used to give us these greaseproof paper twists full of chips and we ate them out there on the grass. I'm sure some of our mates just came round for the chips.'

His Mum glared at his Dad. 'Don't you go encouraging him. I'm not having him eating his meals out there. It's hard enough as it is to get him in here for a square meal these days. There's a slice of toast there, Rob, you're safe enough – Daniel's gate isn't open yet.' Rob checked and ate the toast. He drank his coffee in two gulps. His Mum was still muttering as he left the kitchen.

He ran through the yard and over the cobbles to Daniel's gate. He gave a long, low whistle. Daniel's face appeared at his kitchen window and he was in his yard in seconds. He waved up to his Mum as he closed the gate behind him. The two boys walked over the grass. It was still damp under their feet.

'Did you watch the late film last night?' Rob asked. Daniel shook his head. 'I was tired and Mum said it finished too late,' he said.

'Too late for me too,' Rob said. That was one of the things he liked about Daniel. He didn't pretend he was allowed to do things when he wasn't. It made it easier. His friend Billy from his old place was always talking about what he'd done and what he'd seen on the television and sometimes Rob had agreed that he'd seen the programmes too 'cause he hadn't wanted to seem like a little kid. With Daniel, it was easy to say he'd gone to bed.

They walked over to the skip. It had arrived the day before. The big house on the corner had been sold and the new owners seemed to be cleaning out all sorts of stuff before they moved in properly. It had been flats and the workmen were cleaning it and dumping stuff in the skip. There had been two old-fashioned fireplaces flung in but they'd gone now. Other people must have been interested in the skip too.

The day before there had been an old wooden chest in it and Daniel had taken it home. His Mum had let him keep it. There had been loads of old books and magazines and they'd sifted through them all. Rob had rescued a book which had hundreds of flags of the world in it. He was going to take it to school. His Mum hadn't been keen. She'd gone on about germs and not knowing where things came from but she'd eventually said he could have it.

They climbed up and sat on the edge of the skip. It was almost half full now and there were stones and rubble covering the books that had been there the day before. Daniel couldn't remember who'd lived in the house but he thought that it had been mainly students in flats.

'It'll be good if it's a family who move in,' said Rob, 'with kids.'

'It's a big place,' said Daniel, 'might be too big for just one family. They might be just doing the place up . . . making better flats.'

Rob looked up at the windows. There was no sign of anyone moving in. He looked closely at the

13

house. It wasn't really the end house. There was a little low offshoot which stuck out at the end of it. It was a separate house, much lower than the rest – almost like a basement with nothing above it. It wasn't really part of the big house. Rob tried to see over the back wall but he couldn't get a good look. They both heard the noise at once. A dog. It wasn't barking. It was a sort of whining.

'That's coming from the little house right on the end isn't it?' Rob said. Daniel nodded.

'Sounds like it but I'm not sure who has that one. It might be the old bloke I've seen in the paper shop but I thought he was in one of the flats.' Daniel frowned.

'Did he have a dog?' said Rob.

'He has two,' said Daniel, 'an old dog and one that's just a pup. He occasionally walks them out here on the grass.'

'Seen them lately?' said Rob. Daniel shook his head.

'He's not really that friendly. I've spoken to him once or twice but he's just grunted so I left him to it.'

They both listened. The noise was still there. A whining, half-howling sort of noise.

'Should we check if everything's O.K.?' said Rob.

'How?' said Daniel, 'we can hardly climb the wall and peer in through the windows just because

14

we can hear the dog.'

Rob looked at the wall. 'It might be a good idea,' he said. 'That doesn't sound like a normal noise to me.' Daniel didn't seem too keen. He looked back at his house.

'We can ask my Dad to check if it seems funny,' Rob said. Daniel was happy with that idea.

They stood on the skip and easily reached the wall. They crawled along it, holding on tightly as some of the top bricks were loose and crumbly. The

yard was a mess. The bins hadn't been put out lately and there were bags of rubbish propped up against them.

'What a mess,' said Rob. 'This place needs a good clearing out.'

They jumped down from the wall into the yard. Rob was first to reach the window. He rubbed at the glass to try and see inside. He could hear the dog whining and scratching on the floor or the wall. He moved to the door and tried the handle. It opened. Daniel hung back.

'We'd better not, Rob,' he said. 'There might be trouble if we just barge in.'

'Look, can you let yourself out of the back gate and go to my place. My Dad won't have left yet . . . tell him to come round . . . there's something not right here.'

Daniel nodded. He wasn't all that keen to hang around. Rob pushed the door open and stepped inside. There was a narrow passage-way. It smelt damp. He pushed open the door of the main room. The whining stopped and there was a low growling. Rob felt scared. He didn't really want to go in. He made himself walk in. It was fairly dark in the room but he could see a bed in the corner. There was a person in the bed and a dog lying by the side of the bed. The dog which was growling, was moving towards him with its head down and its ears flat against its head. The figure on the bed didn't move and Rob knew that he was dead. He'd never seen a dead person before but it was so still that he was sure without really looking. He heard his Dad's voice and wanted to move out of the room and run towards the sound. He met him at the door. His Dad grabbed him.

'Take it easy,' Dad said. He looked past Rob into the room. 'I think we're just a bit late for this old bloke.'

Rob felt sick. Dad seemed to know what to do. Daniel was standing by the door. He looked frightened.

Dad looked at the dog on the floor. 'They've both gone,' he said. The other dog had stopped growling. Its tail gave a pathetic wag. Rob reached out to stroke it.

'Take this one home for just now,' Dad said. 'If it doesn't get some food into it, it'll be past it. You've done okay you two, I'll get the police and see to this place. Now hold on to the dog's collar till you're home. The poor animal must be terrified.'

Rob grabbed the collar and led the dog out of the yard. It walked with him without protest. It seemed a friendly sort of dog.

Curly

Rob got up early. He heard his Dad downstairs in the kitchen. That meant he was working another Saturday. He used to moan when there was a lot of weekend work but he didn't seem to bother about it any more. He'd come in last week and he'd seemed quite pleased about going back on Saturday. Rob had mentioned the difference. Dad had grinned. 'Well,' he'd said, 'it's all in a good cause. We didn't think we'd be able to run to the new furniture so quickly but the overtime helps. I've got some incentive now . . . with this place.' Rob had nodded. His Dad was usually in a good mood these days. It was okay.

Rob went down to the kitchen. His Dad was having his breakfast. Skip was lapping milk from his bowl and his tail wagged when Rob walked into the room. Rob patted his head and sat at the table. He pinched a slice of his Dad's toast while he waited for the kettle to boil. Skip leaned against Rob's legs.

'He's been great hasn't he?' said Rob. The dog licked Rob's bare foot. Dad nodded.

'He's a well behaved dog. It was maybe easier getting him when he was that bit older. We didn't have the puppy stage with all the chewing that they

18

do. I don't think we could have convinced your mother if he'd chewed up her carpets.'

'But it would have been awful to get rid of him,' said Rob. 'I mean, he was settled from the moment he came in.'

Dad laughed. 'I think if he'd done any damage, you would have had a hard job talking your Mum into letting you keep him.'

Rob poured some cereal into his bowl. 'Though I have to admit,' said Dad, 'that you look after him pretty well and that's helped it work out.' Skip settled at Rob's feet under the table. Rob watched his Dad wash up his cup and plate.

'Daniel doesn't have a Dad you know,' he said.

Dad sat down at the table. 'Everybody has a Dad, Rob,' he said. 'He just doesn't have his Dad at home . . . but he does have a Dad. He just doesn't live with them.'

'Daniel's seeing him today so he won't be around,' said Rob.

'There you are then,' said Dad.

'What I don't understand is why his Dad can't just come round here and see him and then we could go up the hill with Skip as usual. His Dad could still see him. This way we're losing a day. Daniel won't be back till after tea.'

Dad smiled at him. 'I think you're just going to have to share Daniel today. It's probably quite important to his Dad . . . and you two do get a fair bit of time together. You can't grudge his Dad a bit of his time. Daniel will probably enjoy it too.' Rob grunted.

'Take Skip out and see who turns up,' said Dad. 'Dogs are a bit like babies aren't they . . . people come and talk to you when you're out with one?'

'That's soft,' Rob said. Dad shrugged and pulled on his jacket. Skip walked with him as far as the back door then he sat down and looked hopefully at Rob. Rob took the hint and finished his cereal. He picked up Skip's lead from its peg and the dog jumped around him. They ran up the back lane and took the path up to the hill. Skip knew the way. Once they were safely on to the grassy slope Rob slipped off the lead. He threw the old tennis ball and Skip chased it. He never seemed to get tired of the game. When it was time to go, Rob whistled and the dog bounded back to him and stood waiting for the lead to be clipped on his collar. Rob always remembered. His Dad had been firm about that and anyway he'd seen too many dogs run around free at his old house – they'd been free to get lost and free to be run over.

Rob leaned down and patted Skip's head. He'd waited years to have a dog and now he had Skip it was even better than he'd thought it would be. He wasn't about to take any chances with him.

He stopped when he reached the grass behind the yard. Skip liked to sniff around the trees and poke his nose into the long grass. Rob unwound some of the lead to let him go further. He leaned against the tree just watching the dog. A boy, his age or maybe a bit older, walked over to him.

'That your dog then?' he said. Rob nodded.
'What kind?' the boy asked.
'He's got a bit of bearded collie in him . . . well, he's mostly that,' said Rob.

'That's a funny sort of lead you've got,' the boy said. Rob turned the plastic handle over. 'It's a bit like a fishing line . . . how it works,' he said. 'You can keep him reeled in when you're on the street but you can let him go a bit further when it's safe. My uncle bought it for me when I got the dog.'

'Wouldn't catch me putting a lead on a dog,' the boy said. 'I'd feel stupid. Won't he come to you when you shout?'

'Course he will,' said Rob. 'He's trained but it's safer like this.' The boy didn't look impressed.

'Would he fly at someone if they had a go at you?' the boy said.

'I suppose he might,' said Rob. He'd never thought about it.

'That would be useful,' the boy said.

Rob looked up at Daniel's window. The house looked bare.

'You live around here?' the boy asked. Rob pointed to his house.

'That one there,' he said. 'You live here?'

'Just for now,' the boy said. 'I'm in the home in the middle there but it's what they call short-term. They're moving me on soon . . . they usually do.'

Rob didn't know what to say. He knew there was a sort of Children's Home in the terrace next to his. He and Daniel had met some of the kids when they'd been out on the grass. The ones they'd met had been younger. There had been three girls, two of them sisters and a couple of real youngsters in pedal cars. One of the 'Aunties' had been out keeping an eye on the little ones. They hadn't seen anyone their age.

'My name's Rob,' he said. 'My mate, Daniel, lives over there . . . d'you go to Northmoor?' He didn't recognise the boy from school.

'No chance,' the boy said. 'They're all soft. I go to Eden Terrace . . . that's when I do go . . . which isn't that often. I'm called Curly . . . least that's what my mates call me.' Rob just nodded.

'Will you be living here long?' he asked. He wasn't really sure if he was all that interested.

'Doubt it,' Curly said. 'They never seem to leave me in one place for too long. I don't exactly settle, me, and this place is full of little kids so I don't expect they'll have me there long.'

'That's a shame,' said Rob. He'd only moved once in his whole life and he couldn't think what it would be like to keep moving. Curly shook his head.

'It's not so bad,' he said, 'you get to move on just when they're really sick of you. I think if I hung around too long they'd give up and they'd let fly at me and then I'd have to clout someone.' He pretended to throw a few punches. Skip had found some interesting smells in the grass.

'What do you and your mate do?' he asked.

Rob didn't really want to talk much more. He

wasn't sure why.

'We wander around,' he said, 'play football and go round on our bikes, take the dog up the hill – that sort of thing.'

'Sounds really exciting,' Curly said. Rob knew he was making a fool of them.

'We got Skip when we were out,' he said. 'We heard a noise in one of the houses and we went in. The old man who had him had died. His other dog was dead too.' Curly looked interested.

'You broke in?' he asked. Rob shook his head.

'It wasn't like that,' he said. 'We thought something was wrong so we climbed the wall. The door was open. Skip was whining. That's what we heard.'

'Anything worth nicking – apart from the dog?' Curly said.

'Daniel ran to fetch my Dad,' Rob said. 'It was a bit creepy.' He still remembered it.

'Dead don't harm you,' Curly said, 'and they don't come chasing you either. You two could have cleared the place, and still got the dog.' He was shaking his head. Rob didn't know what to say. He didn't want to sound really stupid. He wanted to go.

'My Dad would have killed me.' He sort of thought that even that might sound stupid to Curly.

'They always say that,' said Curly, 'but they

usually pay the fines all the same.' He shrugged. 'Mine don't even have to do that now so they're not bothered what I do. It doesn't cost me Dad a penny now.'

'Don't you miss being with them?' Rob asked.

'Not specially,' Curly said. 'It was all rows when there was trouble – and I'm always in that.' Rob didn't answer. He fancied going home. He'd find something to do until Daniel came back. He knew he didn't want to hang around with Curly. He wound in Skip's lead.

'I'd better go,' he said. 'I've some things to do for school.' He was using an excuse he was sure Curly wouldn't be interested in.

'You're daft if you do,' said Curly. 'It's just a waste of time.'

'See you,' said Rob and walked to his yard. He sort of hoped he wouldn't see too much of Curly. He felt more comfortable once he was back inside the house.

Moving On

Curly went to the back door of the house. He let himself in and went up the stairs to his room. There were two beds in the room but they didn't have another kid at the moment so he had the room to himself. He looked at the clock on the wall. He had another half-hour before tea. With any luck he hadn't been seen when he came in so they'd likely leave him alone. They were probably still keeping an eye on him. They usually did in the early days. He knew the ropes. He picked up a magazine from his locker and flicked through it. He heard someone ring the bell for tea and went downstairs. He hoped that some of the young kids had been taken out for the weekend. They got on his nerves. Aunty Maureen was on duty. She smiled at him when he walked in.

'Have you been in long?' she asked. 'I didn't see you come in.'

'Came in the back way. Was doing my homework.' He grinned at her.

'Not before time,' she said. 'You know that the school have promised to send a report – on behaviour and your work and everything. It could well help you on the 24th you know.'

'Can't see what difference it'll make,' he said, 'I've already been put away haven't I?' He pulled a face.

'That's all you know,' she said. 'There are worse places than this for your information.' He shrugged.

'Like places where you don't get out at all and you don't go to your own school with your own mates and where you get no freedom at all,' Aunty Maureen went on. She smiled at him. 'Come on, Curly,' she said. 'It's not that bad here and you know it; if you make a go of it maybe things will get straightened out. Once you're settled and there's no problems then you could be on the way to being back at home. That's what everybody wants isn't it?'

'Any chance of more beans?' he said.

She put an extra spoonful on his plate. 'I sometimes think it's a waste of time talking to you,' she said. 'You don't give much away do you?'

He sat down at the table. After Aunty Maureen had finished serving the meal, she brought her plate over to his table.

'You've been out a fair bit this weekend Curly,' she said. He nodded.

'So where did you go?' she asked. She was still smiling.

'Out,' he said.

'Have it your own way,' she said.

'Well there's hardly a lot to do around here,' he

said, 'so you needn't worry.'

She drank her coffee. 'So what's wrong with round here?' she said. 'The other kids play on the grass out the back and there are usually kids your age around. I've seen them out on their bikes.'

'I'm too big for your pedal cars and the kids that live here seem pretty useless.' He took an extra slice of bread from the tray.

'I suppose you know them?' she said.

'Matter of fact,' he said, 'I met one of them yesterday. A kid out the back there with his dog. I talked to him for a while. It wasn't a bad dog he had either – apart from him fussing around making sure it was on a lead . . . and he goes to Northmoor and you know what they're like . . . dead soft all of them . . . they get in trouble if they don't have their ties on . . . catch me walking around with a tie on . . . they must be really soft.'

Aunty Maureen didn't say anything for a bit. 'Remember, if you make any friends out there, Curly, it's okay to bring them back here. You can make a cup of coffee in the kitchen and there are usually biscuits in the tin. Whoever's on duty won't mind if it's just someone you've met out the back. It would probably be good for you to get a friend from around here.'

'Wouldn't want one,' he said.

'It would still be nice,' she said.

He shifted in his seat. 'The one I met was so

soft,' he said, 'he and his mate found this house with an old guy dead in it and they got his Dad to see to it. That's how he got his dog. It was in the house. They could have had what they wanted but they were so scared they got his Dad . . . really soft that is.'

'They were being sensible,' she said, 'but I don't suppose you're interested in that.' She picked up her cup and stood up. He gathered up his dishes and put them down next to the sink.

'Want to give Lisa a hand with the dishes?' she asked.

'No chance,' he said. 'It's not my turn.' He went towards the door. 'Okay if I go out to the shop later?' he asked, 'I've got some money.'

'Won't it be shut?' she said.

'It stops open till nine,' he said. 'I just want some crisps.'

She thought for a moment. 'Okay, but don't be too long.'

'I'm not one of the little kids,' he said, 'I can look after myself you know,' and slammed the door as he left. He picked up some money from his room and left by the back door. He walked over the cobbles, kicking some loose stones and an empty tin can. Sometimes he got really sick of them fussing. When he'd been at home no one had checked where he was going . . . he'd just pleased himself . . . and he'd had mates . . . better mates than the soft kids around here . . . mates who wouldn't have turned down the chance of a house with only an old dead man inside.

Curly sighed. They'd never taken a thing that pair . . . and who'd have known? He stopped and leaned against the tree then swung up so that he could sit on one of the broad branches. He heard a dog bark. Then the two kids came along the back lane. The other one was holding the lead. He looked pleased with himself. Curly whistled. The kid he'd met waved and spoke to the other one. Then they turned into one of the yards. Curly frowned then shrugged. They could please themselves . . . he wasn't bothered. He looked around the triangle of grass. There was nothing to do. He looked at the cars parked down the end under the trees. One car caught his eye. It was smart. One of those all white jobs – white wheel trims, the lot. He wondered if he should pop the badges off it. Big Mick at school was saving badges. Then he saw the sun roof. It was open. He was interested. It was worth a look. He swung down from the tree and walked over, not looking at the car as he walked. He looked over his shoulder to the windows of the home. They'd still be getting the little kids settled. No one would be bothering about him. He walked past the car then leaned against the tree nearest it. He could see inside. Really smart it was – red and black seats and a thick leather steering wheel. It

probably belonged to a right big head. He checked
the back seat . . . didn't seem to be much worth
taking . . . a pair of shoes and a sweater. Then he
saw the tapes . . . about twenty or so . . . on the
passenger seat. He waited. He couldn't make out
what they were. They were good ones though. Not
copies . . . *someone* would want them. They were all
bright colours and neat. They'd look sharp on his
shelf. He could say he'd got them as a present. His
brother, Billy, would be sure to back him up. He'd
give Billy some of them.

He could hear his heart thumping. He was out of practice. It would be better with a mate. But there wasn't one, so it would have to be a solo job.

He jumped down and moved in close to the car and put his hand into the gap between the sunroof and the frame. He pulled it and it opened wider. Not wide enough. There was a stick on the ground. He picked it up and used it to force the catch. It gave, and the glass sunroof came out from its clips. The stick shot from his hand and banged against the paintwork. There were marks on the roof but he was just looking at the tapes. He leaned inside and grabbed a handful. He stuffed them inside his jacket. He'd get a plastic carrier down at the shop. He cleared the seat. A couple of cassettes rattled on to the ground. There wasn't time to be tidy. He zipped his jacket and slid down from the roof. His trainer caught on a lamp and it broke off. Serves the bloke right – they were probably just for show. He ran to the lane, the tapes banging around inside his jacket.

Once he had got his breath, he went to the shop. He bought his crisps and a plastic bag. The man charged him for the bag. He'd nick some sweets next time to make up for it. He loaded his tapes into the bag and zipped up his jacket. Turning into the back lane, he nearly bumped into two policemen. One blocked his way and the other took his carrier bag from him. He swore.

Daniel looked out of his window. Rob was just getting some comics he was going to borrow.

'There are a couple of panda cars out the back,' he said. Rob came to look.

One car was parked on the grass. A policeman was taking notes and talking to a man who was leaning on a white car. Two other policemen were walking to the other car with a lad between them. Rob recognised Curly.

Strangers

Daniel leaned on his windowsill. There was still rain on the glass and he looked out at the puddles on the car-park. It wasn't falling anymore but it didn't look fine enough to be out. Rob was fiddling with the record player. Skip was at home. They'd get a chance to take him up the hill later if it stopped raining.

'Typical,' said Daniel. 'It's fine all week then it rains on a Friday night . . .' Rob nodded.

'I had the dog out early this morning and it was great – really bright, but it clouded over while we were in Maths today.'

'Typical,' said Daniel. He looked again out of his window just to check.

'That kid's out on his bike,' he said. Rob looked up.

'What kid?' he asked.

'The house with the blue paint,' Daniel said. 'He's out now and again. He goes to that school where they wear the caps . . . must feel a right idiot . . . I saw him around last summer before you came. They had caps on in the summer term too.'

'What's he like?' said Rob.

Daniel grunted. 'He's okay I suppose. Sometimes he has one of his mates with him but I've never really met him properly 'cause his holidays are different and he's not often out on a night. They don't finish till late. He said they do their homework in the school so he doesn't get back till late. It must be rotten.'

Rob nodded. He closed the lid of the turntable.

'When we were in the Juniors, a kid in my class went to a school like that,' Rob said. 'He was brainy. We didn't see him again after he left . . . don't know what happened to him.'

Daniel laughed. 'You've maybe passed him in town and didn't know it was him. He'd be talking proper. Maybe in Latin or French or something.' They both laughed.

'Is that kid there snobby?' asked Rob.

Daniel shook his head. 'I've not noticed . . . don't think so,' he said.

'Seems nice enough.'

'Must be just brainy,' Rob said. He pulled a face. They laughed again. When the rain stopped, they raced back to Rob's and got Skip. He was ready for his run up the hill.

The kid from the blue house was going round the cobbles on his bike when they walked over the grass. He looked over towards them. Daniel waved and shouted 'Hello'. Rob had just got Skip's lead fixed. He was keen to be away.

'Going for a walk?' the kid said.

Daniel nodded. Rob looked at the kid before they turned the corner. He wasn't sure if he really fancied talking to him. He was a bit younger than them. Rob didn't know if they'd have much to talk to him about anyway. He was glad when they were out of sight.

'He's not that bad you know,' said Daniel. 'I hung around with him a bit last holidays.'

'I didn't say he was,' said Rob. 'You go if you want to get back.' As soon as he'd said it he felt stupid. He didn't seem able to stop himself. 'If you're quick you can catch the kid on his bike,' he added.

'What's got into you?' said Daniel.

'I just don't want to drag you away. You said you'd never met that kid properly. Now you're saying you hung about with him a bit . . . so maybe you'd best get back. He looked keen enough. Your mother would probably quite like you to be mates with a kid like that.' He started to walk faster.

Daniel looked surprised. 'What's brought this on. You in a mood about something?' he asked.

'Just leave it,' Rob said, 'I'll see you.' He pulled in Skip's lead and walked towards the roundabout and the path to the hill. Daniel hung back then turned towards home. He didn't say anything.

Rob took Skip up the hill by the usual path. He threw the old tennis ball and Skip brought it back. Rob's heart wasn't in it though and Skip seemed to

have an idea that something was wrong. He didn't
bark or run about. He kept coming back and just
sitting at Rob's feet. Rob leaned against the old
stone wall. He felt sick. He didn't know why he'd
had a go at Daniel. They were mates after all. They
did all sorts of things together and if he really
thought about it, it wasn't very likely that Daniel
would just leave him and go off with somebody else.
The idea seemed to make him angry and he didn't
like it. It was like when Daniel had to spend the day
with his Dad. He didn't know Daniel's Dad, but he
had sort of decided that he didn't like him. He'd
spoiled their day. By the time he'd thought about it
for a bit, he felt bad. He didn't want to remember
how he was feeling. It was a bit like being caught
when you'd done something wrong. His face felt
hot. He whistled to Skip and they headed back
down towards the road. He felt funny about turning into the back lane. He wasn't sure what he'd do
if Daniel was there. He wanted to get home and
leave it all till the morning. Maybe everything
would be better then.

Daniel wasn't anywhere around. There was no
one on the grass and there didn't seem to be any
bikes around. Rob walked quickly. Then he saw
the three of them. The boy from the blue house
with his bike and two other lads. The two boys were
older. They looked like they were Rob's age. They
were standing with the boy. Rob looked away.

Probably friends of the kid's. Then he looked back. Something was wrong. They didn't seem to be friends. They were standing next to the kid in a funny way. One was in front of his bike and the other was at the side of him. He looked scared. They were laughing and calling him names.

Rob slowed down. He heard one of them swearing. The kid didn't seem to be saying anything at all. They were making a fool of him and pushing him. One of them kicked the back wheel of the bike. Rob didn't really take time to think.

All at once he remembered what the boy, Curly, had said to him. Something about 'if someone set about you would your dog go for them?' Rob didn't know. He walked over towards them. The two bigger boys were grinning. The kid looked really worried. Rob wished he knew his name. He decided to behave like he knew him. He shouted

'Hello'. The kid joined in and looked pleased to see him. Rob let Skip's lead fall away. He walked over to the kid and said, 'We going back to your place now?' The kid caught on. He moved his bike.

'We didn't say you could go,' one of the boys said. He put his hand on Rob's arm. There was a low growl. They all looked at Skip. He was showing his teeth and his fur was standing up on the back of his neck. He wasn't having it. The boy stepped back. Skip was still growling.

'Let's leave them to it,' the other boy said. The growling went on. The boys turned away, slowly at first then they ran off towards the cut, calling names as they ran.

Neither Rob nor the kid said anything.

'Doubt if they'll be back,' Rob said. He felt sort of grown-up.

The kid smiled at him. 'Thanks for that,' he said. 'I thought I was going to get a black eye or lose my bike . . . they just appeared out of nowhere.'

'Well,' said Rob, 'Skip didn't think much of them.'

'He's a great dog,' the boy said. 'You're really lucky to have him. I've watched him from the window, he's very well trained . . . never puts a foot wrong.'

Rob felt quite proud. 'He's good is Skip. He seems to know most things you say to him.' Skip wagged his tail.

Rob felt stupid again. The kid didn't seem at all bad. It was Rob who'd picked the row with Daniel and here he was standing with the kid talking about Skip and Daniel wasn't even around.

'What are you called?' said Rob.

'Richard,' the kid said.

'I'm Rob. I live over there,' he pointed.

Richard nodded. 'Thanks again anyway. I'd probably better get home.'

Daniel's back gate opened and he came out on to the grass. Rob wanted to call over to him. Richard moved first. He called Daniel over and told him what had happened. Rob thought that he had been made to sound braver and tougher than he'd actually been. Daniel grinned.

'I can see you've already met my mate Rob, then.'

Rob suddenly felt a lot better. He'd probably say he was sorry later on. Richard looked at his watch. 'I have to go,' he said. He looked as if he would rather stay.

'We'll see you again then,' said Rob. The kid grinned and nodded.

Daniel and Rob went back to the house. 'Good programme on at eight,' Rob said.

'You're on,' said Daniel. Skip followed them.

Girl Talk

'Ever thought about girls?' Rob said.

Daniel looked up. 'How d'you mean?' he said. Rob jumped from the tree and landed on the grass beside Richard and Daniel.

'Like why they don't live here,' he said.

'Rob wants a girl,' said Daniel, 'or maybe three or four. Come on, Rich, we'd better look for some for him.'

Rob flung some grass at him. 'Don't be soft,' he said. 'I'm being serious. I was just looking round at the houses and it dawned on me that we're all boys . . . shut up you two . . . think about it. There don't seem to be many girls around here. I just wondered why it was.'

Richard and Daniel were still laughing.

'There aren't any girls in my school,' Richard said.

'There are loads in ours,' said Daniel.

'We don't have a sister, any of us,' said Rob.

Daniel thought about it. 'Suppose you're right in a way . . . we don't have brothers either. It's probably just one of those daft things that we just happen to have got together and none of us has a sister or a brother for that matter. There's no reason . . .

I don't think.' Rob kept on. 'But we all hang around out here . . . but I've never seen a girl out here.'

'When the little kids are out it's different,' said Daniel. 'There are the young kids from the home and that pair from the end. When I get in from school there's often a whole load of them out here with their toys. They all go in a lot earlier though and they're not out early in the morning so we don't see much of them.'

'I don't think it's just that,' said Rob.

'I was just wondering how many girls live around here that we don't see . . . out here.'

'There's the girl in the house nearest the lane,' said Richard.

'Big Bertha,' Daniel whispered to Rob. They both laughed. Richard looked puzzled.

'She's in the fifth year at our school,' said Daniel. 'She's a prefect.'

'She's two prefects,' said Rob, 'and she's not likely to knock around out here on her bike.'

Daniel giggled. 'I can just see Big Bertha on a bike . . .'

'There are two girls in the house with the trees in the yard,' Richard said.

'You don't miss much young Richard,' said Rob. He tried to sound serious. Richard threw some grass at him.

'That's what you were saying though,' said

Daniel. 'They live just there,' he pointed at the house, 'but they just walk through here on the way to school. They don't come out here of a night or at the weekend.'

'Maybe not allowed to,' said Richard.

'That's what I mean,' said Rob. 'Why?'

'Girls do different things,' said Richard.

'How come you're such an expert,' said Daniel, 'since you don't have any at all at your school?'

'I just think they do,' Richard said. 'Anyway, I didn't start this . . . it was *his* idea.' He looked at Rob.

'It wasn't so much an idea really,' said Rob, 'but where I used to live, some of the girls hung around with the rest of us but I haven't seen so many . . . well like none . . . around here. That's all I was doing . . . just wondering.'

'You could go and ask them if they fancy a game of football,' Daniel giggled. 'Best of luck.'

'You two are being stupid,' said Rob. 'I was just looking around and sort of thinking. I wasn't about to do anything about it.'

'Girls are different,' Daniel said. Rob and Richard laughed this time.

'You know what I mean,' he said. 'The younger ones play with other girls, dolls and houses and all that and then . . . well, after that . . . I don't think they play much for a while, then they're into the cafe in town or maybe they stay in and get their work done. I don't know. Most of the girls in my class seem to get their work done no bother . . . so I don't suppose they've anything better to do. Their Mums probably expect them to be in of an evening. I don't know.'

'There are a few in our school who are always in bother, Dan,' said Rob.

'Ally Robson is wicked and that lot who hang around with Julie Page are always in trouble . . . real sort of serious trouble.'

'They just like to show off,' Daniel said. 'Nobody really has much to do with them.'

'I know kids who are scared of that lot,' said Rob. Daniel shrugged.

'I'd never really thought about it before,' said Rob, 'but there must be a real sort of difference in the way they think.'

'How's that?' Daniel said.

'Well,' Rob continued, 'if there wasn't, there'd be a couple of girls out here now . . . we'd be knocking around with them and . . .'

'Then they'd be *girlfriends*,' Daniel laughed, 'not mates . . . anyway it depends what sort of girl you're talking about.'

'What sort of girl?' Rob said.

Daniel nodded. 'Well there are girly girls who play out when they're little then get sort of grown up and don't play out, but there are girls like the ones you said, who run around with the lads and climb and everything. They're just like boys really and you never think of them as girls . . . they're usually a bit wild though. There was a girl who used to live up in the next terrace . . . she came out here with her big brother. Terri, she was called . . . great footballer and all but she was just like a boy . . . wanted to be a mechanic . . . bit bossy but not like most of the girls I know.'

'Girls can be mechanics,' said Richard, 'and lorry drivers and secret agents. The plumber who fixed our sink was a girl . . . well a woman.'

'Not many do though,' said Daniel, 'so I don't think it's that popular . . . not with most girls.'

'It's because of the difference. It makes sense what I've been saying,' said Rob. 'At least, I think it does.' He frowned. 'Glad you've got it all worked out.'

Daniel laughed. 'You must be relieved.' Rob jumped up and swung on the branch of the tree.

'I'm sure we're better climbers,' he said.

Richard looked up at him. 'The girl gymnasts are great,' he said. 'They swing on the bars and just fly through the air.' Rob swung higher. The other two smiled at him.

Suddenly, he cried out and let the branch go. He fell hard on to the ground and curled over with his hand tucked into his armpit.

'So much for the expert,' said Daniel.

'Come on Rob . . . get up.'

They saw Rob's white face and the blood spreading over his sweater from where he was holding his hand. They both got up.

'You okay?' asked Richard. 'What did you do?'

'Caught my hand on something.' Rob was speaking quietly. 'Felt a sharp bit and just let go . . . feels horrible.' He didn't want to move. He kept his hand stuck under his other arm.

'Let's have a look,' said Daniel. Rob didn't seem

keen but he slowly drew his hand out.

There was a deep cut in the soft skin at the base of his thumb. Blood was pouring from it and as he moved his hand the cut seemed to get wider.

'I feel sick,' he said, 'and my Mum won't be in yet . . . it's late shopping.' Richard seemed to know what to do.

'Come on,' he said. 'My Mum's in. I'll run and tell her.' Richard ran to his house and Rob and Daniel followed. There was blood dripping on to Rob's jeans. His face was very white. Daniel didn't feel too good either.

Richard's Mum met them at the door. She put her arm round Rob's shoulder and wrapped a clean white tea towel around his hand. He felt better when he couldn't see the cut.

'It's up to the hospital for you,' she said. 'We can't be sure if there's any dirt in that cut and it would be best if a doctor looked at it.'

She put all three boys in the car. 'We'll probably be home before your Mum gets back,' she said. Rob thought it would be good to be home.

There weren't many people in the waiting room at the hospital but Rob was taken right away. He sat on the bed. It was hard and high. His hand was still wrapped up. A man in a white coat came in and took the towel off Rob's hand.

'What were you doing?' the man asked.

'Swinging on the tree,' Rob said. 'We were talking about girls and I was showing my friends that boys are better at climbing than girls.' The young man smiled and cleaned the cut. It was still bleeding.

'I'll tidy this up but I think you'll need a stitch. Doctor will be here in a minute.'

'Aren't you a doctor?' asked Rob.

'I'm a nurse,' said the man.

Rob looked at him in surprise. 'We were talking about that sort of thing,' he said. The man smiled at him. 'I'd just worked out that girls are different,' said Rob, 'and now I come here and you're a nurse. I thought girls were nurses.'

The man laughed. 'Here's something else for you to think about then. Dr Wallace will stitch up your cut and give you an injection in case you got any dirt in this.'

Dr Wallace smiled at Rob.

'How did you do this then?' she asked.

Rob just looked at her. 'I'm not really sure,' he said.

Camping Out

'Richard's got a tent you know,' Rob said. His Mum and Dad didn't say anything.

'It's a proper tent,' said Rob. 'It was his Dad's but it's Richard's now. He used to play in it on the grass but it's a proper tent so you could actually camp in it.'

His Dad looked at him. 'So?' he said.

'I thought maybe the three of us could camp out some time . . . just for the night. We could take some food and things and sleep the night in the tent,' he said.

'When you three get together, it can end up with one of you at the hospital,' his Mum said, 'and I'd rather it wasn't you again.'

Rob sighed. 'That was just an accident,' he said. 'It wasn't serious.'

His Mum shook her head. 'Oh no, it wasn't serious,' she said. 'I come home to find you've been carted off to the General and had eight stitches and you've got your arm in a sling . . . and you were just playing outside the yard. I dread to think what you'd do if you were further away.'

'That sort of thing can happen, love,' his Dad said. 'Lads climb trees and sometimes, like Rob, they take a tumble. I remember when I was about his age, Alex and I were building a rope swing and . . .'

'That's not the point,' his Mum said, 'and I don't want to hear what you and Alex did. I'm always surprised you two managed to grow up at all, the things you got up to. It was me who had to come home and find no sign of Rob. The one night I go out to get the shopping and then I get back to find nobody here. Then Richard's Mum brings him back with his face as white as a sheet and he's all bandages and they've been at the General and there was I doing my shopping while he was lying out on the street, hurt.'

'I wasn't lying on the street,' said Rob. 'It was just a cut and Richard's Mum didn't mind. She was really good about it.'

'That's not the point either,' Mum said.

'It's a great tent,' Rob said. 'We could easily camp out just one night or so up the hill. Skip could come with us. We'd be okay with him.'

'A lot of good a dog would be if you were hurt,' Mum said.

'I'll feel a right idiot if I'm the only one who's not allowed to go,' Rob said. He looked at his Dad.

'How would you have felt?' he said. 'I mean, Rich is just a kid and if his Dad and Mum say it's fine for him, what am I supposed to say?' His Dad gave him that look. The one that meant 'Leave it, but maybe'.

'Your Mum and I will talk about this,' he said. Rob left it. That was often the best way. He went off to bed.

He met the other two outside the next day.

'Did you ask about camping out?' said Daniel.

Rob nodded. 'Mum wasn't dead keen,' he said, 'but I think Dad would let me. He and Uncle Alex used to, so I'll maybe ask again.'

Daniel frowned. 'My Mum wasn't too keen either but I sort of hinted that you were going to be able to do it and she said she'd think about it . . . that means she wasn't saying no.'

Richard looked pleased. 'I said I'd be with you two and I think they thought you'd be sensible enough 'cause you're older than I am. My Mum thinks you're quite grown up,' he said.

'We might just swing it,' Rob said.

Richard laughed. 'My Mum thought I was talking about camping out here on the grass and she was okay about it when she thought she'd be able to keep an eye on me from the window.' He pulled a face.

'Did you tell her we were thinking of the Priory?' said Daniel.

Richard looked down. 'Not really,' he said. 'I said we were hoping to go to the hill.'

'That's just up the road,' said Daniel. 'That's hardly camping out.' Richard didn't say anything.

'I think mine would just about accept the hill,' Rob said, 'but I really don't think the Priory is on. My Mum would say no . . . I'm pretty sure.'

Daniel sighed. 'Fine then, it's the hill. It's better than nothing I suppose. We'll all work on that.'

By the end of the week it had more or less been agreed. Richard's Mum had talked to Rob's Mum and the boys had been told that they could do it . . . but just for the one night and Skip was going too. They made their plans. Rob borrowed a sleeping bag from his cousin and Richard got one from a boy at school. Daniel had one of his own. He slept in it now and again when he had people staying with him. He'd never camped with it properly before.

The night before they were due to leave, they met at Rob's house.

'Wish we'd tried the idea of the Priory,' said Daniel. 'It would seem more like an adventure . . . a lad I know, his brother and his mates go there in the holidays. They take their bikes and stay for about a week. There's a good area for camping just beyond the old abbey.'

'Give over Dan,' said Rob. 'There's no way my folk, well my Mum, would have gone for the idea of the Priory. She'd have gone on about us having accidents or something. Maybe if we can show everybody we can manage, then when it's the holidays . . . well, it might be different then.'

'My Mum's still not dead pleased that she won't be able to see me from the window. If she drives up to the hill just to check on me I'll go mad. I've told her not to but . . .' He didn't seem too sure.

'Haven't you been away from home?' Daniel asked.

'Course I have,' said Richard. 'I often stay overnight with my friend and I've been to my Aunt's in Scotland . . . on my own. I've been with the school too. We went to a sort of cabin and did some climbing and canoeing.'

'Your Mum was okay about us going,' said Rob.

'Well, she's not sure,' Richard admitted, 'and she keeps telling me not to do anything stupid but . . . I think Rob's right. If we use this trip to prove what we can do, then we can get round to doing whatever we want to . . . even the Priory.'

'What could we do that would be stupid up at the hill,' Daniel said.

'I mean it's so near, they'd hear us if we made too much noise,' Richard giggled.

Rob laughed. 'Come on,' he said, 'that lot from our class who camped out last year . . . they had all that home-made beer and then they went down on to the beach. There was quite a bit of trouble.'

'Were they arrested?' said Richard.

'That was the sort of thing my Mum was going on about,' he added.

'They weren't arrested,' said Rob. 'There was just some trouble . . . anyway, they were real idiots. Some of them get into trouble even when they're at home and sleeping in their own beds so I don't think it made a big difference . . . they were just daft.'

'Do we have everything we need?' asked Daniel.

'We've all got sleeping bags,' said Rob, 'and we've got the tent.'

'What about food?' said Richard.

'I thought we could take some sandwiches and a few bottles of pop,' Rob said.

'Aren't we even going to cook?' Daniel shrugged. 'Great camping trip this is going to be.'

'Cook on what?' Richard asked.

'A fire or a stove,' Daniel said. 'That's why it's called a campfire, idiot. We could do baked potatoes and sausages and maybe beans.' Rob and Richard didn't look too sure.

'It would be a lot to carry, just up the hill,' Rob grinned, 'and I'm not too sure about making a fire up there.'

'My Mum would go mad,' Richard said quietly.

'Don't be daft,' Daniel said. 'She'd see the glow from your top window.'

They decided to meet first thing in the morning to check that they had everything they needed.

When Rob woke, he heard the rain. The wind was blowing it hard against his window. He pulled his quilt up over his shoulders. It was cold too. After

breakfast Daniel and Richard came round and they sat in the kitchen having some tea. Rob passed a jar of biscuits around.

Daniel's wet parka hung on the back of the chair. Richard's anorak was dripping on the floor.

'The weather's let us down a bit,' Daniel said. He took another biscuit.

'The grass is like a swamp,' said Richard. 'It's just mud all over the place.'

'Don't think we'll get a fire going tonight,' said Rob. The other two agreed.

'What's the forecast?' he asked.

'More rain,' Richard said. 'I checked the television when I got up.' They didn't speak for a while. The rain ran down the window.

Rob took a deep breath. 'Think we're going to have to leave it tonight,' he said, 'because if we get really soaked, they'll not be too keen on the real trip next time.' He waited for them to say something. They both seemed quite pleased.

'Think I'll sleep in my sleeping bag anyway,' said Daniel. 'I'll set it out on the floor.'

Tidying Up

Rob was kicking a ball against the wall. He was the only one out. He knew one of the others would come out soon so he hung around. Skip watched the ball hit the wall. He knew he wasn't allowed to chase that ball. He picked up his old ball and looked up at Rob. The boy laughed at him, put his leather ball down on the grass and threw Skip's ball off over the cobbles. The dog moved between the little children who were playing on the flat concrete behind the patch of grass. One of the Mums walked over to Rob.

'Your dog's good with the little ones isn't he?' she said. 'I often watch him. My little boy thinks he's great.' Rob smiled. Everyone seemed to like Skip.

'He likes little kids,' he said, 'and he knows not to jump up on them. He's never been any bother.'

The woman stood with him and chatted to him. 'It's nice for them out here,' she said, 'but I still don't like to leave them. I'll be glad when mine can play out here by themselves but I don't think it'll be this year. It'll be different when they're your age,' she laughed.

'Not much can happen to them out here,' Rob said.

'You're not a three-year-old and I bet when you were, your Mum kept a good eye on you,' she said. Rob couldn't remember being three but he thought she might be right. They watched the kids play on their push along bikes.

'There's quite a gang there,' Rob said.

The woman nodded. 'The twins there are from the Children's Home. They're playing with my little girl. The boy on the little tractor is mine and the other two live two doors down from me. That's their Mum painting the window in their yard.'

'They'll be the next lot to play out here like we do,' Rob said.

'You'll probably be away with kids of your own by then,' she said. Rob laughed at this.

Another yard gate opened and they watched another little one trot out on to the concrete.

'He's not so sure whether he wants to play or not,' Rob said.

'That's Beth,' the woman said. 'She's not out often. She's been ill.' She spoke quietly.

'Looks like a boy,' Rob said, 'with that short haircut. She's nearly bald.'

The woman nodded. 'The treatment made her hair fall out. She's been ill for months. She must be a little better since she's out.' She moved away. 'I'll go and keep an eye on her, poor little thing.'

Rob picked up Skip's ball and went towards Richard's yard. He looked back at the little girl. She was thinner and paler than the others and she didn't rush around like most of them. She looked different. He banged on Richard's back door. His Mum answered. She smiled at Rob.

'Go on up. He's clearing out some shelves in his room before he disappears under all the mess.'

Rob wasn't sure he wanted to be in on the clearing up. Richard's Mum seemed to catch on. She took two cans from the fridge and handed him a couple of packets of crisps.

'You can keep him company,' she said, 'but I want to be able to see my way into that room before he tries to leave the house so don't you help him break out.' She was smiling, so Rob thanked her and went upstairs. He didn't know Richard's Mum that well. She was always nice to him but he never knew what to say to her. She wasn't like his Mum. She wore fairly modern clothes for a Mum and she spoke in a bit of a posh voice. She'd been great when he'd hurt himself and she'd taken him to the hospital and everything but she reminded him of some of his teachers at school and he sort of behaved like that with her. He always remembered to say 'thank you' and he spoke sort of properly to her. She often spoke to Richard as if he was a grown-up. They talked about all sorts of things and Rob was sometimes a bit worried that she'd talk to him about something that was going on in the world and he wouldn't know what to say. Still, she always seemed pleased to see him and she seemed to like him playing with Richard. She often had ice-cream or pop or something ready for both of them. She didn't mind when all three of them stopped for tea and she'd just laughed when Skip had eaten up all the cat food in the dish on their kitchen floor. She was fine really, just different from his own Mum.

Rob pushed open Richard's door. Richard was pleased to see him.

'I'd have been out,' he said, 'but I had to get this place tidied up.' He was throwing bits of paper into a black plastic bin bag.

'Every now and then,' he said, 'Mum has a fit and decides that my room is a mess. It's taking me longer than I thought it would. You can give Skip that chocolate. I found it under some books. It's months old but he won't care.' Skip didn't mind.

Rob sat on the blue chair while Richard worked. The room was looking quite tidy. Rob didn't think it would take long.

'I was talking to a woman out on the grass,' Rob said, 'and there's one of the kids out there who's been ill. She's really bald with the treatment she's been having. I thought she was a lad. I felt stupid.'

'That'll be Beth,' Richard said.

Rob nodded. 'That's right,' he said. 'D'you know about her?'

'I've heard people talking about it,' Richard

said. 'She's got a blood disease. She was really bad about Christmas time and nobody expected her to get better. My Mum gets quite upset about her. It's bad when it's a young kid.'

'How d'you mean?' said Rob. 'Is she still so bad?'

Richard shrugged. 'I'm not sure but I don't think she'll get better. I mean *really* better. I think she'll just have times when she's a bit better . . . but I don't think she'll . . . well . . . you know.'

Rob nodded. They didn't say anything for a while.

'It must be awful,' Rob said. Richard looked up. He nodded. He slung some comics into the plastic bag.

'I mean,' said Rob, 'she'll maybe never be our age.'

Richard leaned back against the bed. He gave Skip the bits of crisps at the bottom of the bag. Rob watched them.

'I wouldn't like to have died when I'd just been a kid,' he said.

'You wouldn't have known what you'd missed,' Richard said. 'I think . . . I mean . . . how could you have . . . if you'd died when you'd been young. It would have been your Mum and Dad who would have been in a state. It wouldn't have made a lot of difference to you would it?'

Rob took a drink from his can. 'It's still hard to

think about isn't it?' he said.

'If you'd been like that?' Richard said.

'No,' said Rob, 'dying and that sort of thing.'

Richard put the books in a neat pile on the shelf. 'I'm not dead keen on thinking about it,' he said. They both laughed at his words.

'Daniel and I found that old bloke who had Skip,' Rob said. 'He was dead. I knew he was as soon as I walked into that room. He was still and there was a sort of funny feel about the place. I was glad my Dad came then. I didn't want to hang around I can tell you.'

Richard leaned back again. 'It's funny that, isn't it, 'cause a dead person isn't really going to hurt you.'

Rob shrugged. Richard often sounded like an older person.

'Have you ever seen a dead person?' he asked Richard.

The boy shook his head. 'My Grandad died but he was in hospital and my other Grandma died when I was just a baby.'

'D'you think that little girl knows . . . about how ill she is?' Rob said.

'I don't know,' Richard said. 'My Mum said that when little kids are really ill, they're often great about it . . . they seem to, you know, not mind too much.' He tied the black plastic sack with a wire.

'It's really rotten isn't it,' Rob said. 'It just doesn't seem right. She's just a little kid. I've always thought of dying being for really old folk.'

'There are earthquakes and bombs and plane crashes and wars,' said Richard. 'It's always on the news.'

'I know that,' Rob said, 'but a lot of them are accidents and everybody knows that they can just happen. A gas pipe could blow us all up, even a whole class of us at school, but you know these things can just happen. You don't ever really think about them. Somebody our age or younger than us getting so ill that they die is different. It makes me feel funny.'

Richard didn't answer. He pushed the books into a tidy pile on his shelf. 'That should keep my Mum happy,' he said. 'I should be okay to get out now. What about a walk up the hill with Skip? I've got some money. We could get an ice-cream at the paper shop.'

'You're on,' said Rob. He jumped up and Skip seemed to know there was going to be a walk in it for him.

'If I was really ill I'd miss Sunday dinners and trifle most of all,' Rob said.

'Fruit and nut chocolate for me,' Richard said.

Mrs Baxter

The weather had been fine for days. Mrs Baxter looked out of her kitchen window. She'd be able to do a few hours in the backyard. Some of her white pots needed weeding and the plant which grew up the wall had to be cut back. Maybe if it stayed fine and she didn't get too tired . . .

She washed up her breakfast dishes. She still liked to have a proper breakfast sitting at the table in the kitchen. She always used her yellow cup and saucer and the yellow egg cup for her boiled egg. Most people thought it was silly to set the table and go to any trouble just for one but she'd always done it. When Sam had been working and the children were at home, they'd always sat in the kitchen round the big wooden table for a proper family breakfast. They'd all talked about what they'd be doing that day and then young Colin would run to the door when a letter rattled through the letter-box. He'd liked getting the mail and would bring it through to the kitchen for his Dad.

Once the children had grown up and left, she and Sam had taken it slowly at breakfast time and after he retired, they left it quite late and some days she even made a second pot of tea while Sam put a few more slices of bread under the grill. They often got a letter from Colin when he was at college or a postcard from Elizabeth when she was working abroad. They'd enjoyed these mornings. When Sam died, she'd never really thought about changing her morning routine. For a while, Colin wrote more often than he had before and Elizabeth found time to write a proper letter instead of a picture postcard. She always saved them until her second cup of tea when she could sit and read them, maybe more than once, and then put them into her big cardboard file that she had once used for recipes. She sighed. She didn't get so much post these days. It seemed to be bills more than anything else. Elizabeth was living in America and didn't seem to have much time to write a proper long letter. She got quick notes and she still got excited when she saw the foreign stamp. Elizabeth liked to be called Liz now and she had a good job. She'd sent a tape once and Mrs Baxter had gone round to her friend's house and had listened to it on her friend's grandson's machine. She'd been able to hear her daughter's voice telling her all about her job and her flat. She'd felt a bit awkward about listening to it with folk there and hadn't really been able to go over it again and again as she didn't have one of the machines.

Colin kept in touch. He didn't write so many letters now but he sent the children's school photographs and holiday snaps and he phoned to check that she was fine. She was very lucky really. Some people had no one. She was well enough to keep her little garden tidy and when it was sunny she opened up the back gates and sat in her seat looking out on to the grass at the back of the houses. She liked to watch the little ones play. She remembered being out there when Colin and Elizabeth were little. She'd often hung out her washing and watched her two playing out under the same trees that the little ones were playing under now. It had been safer then. There hadn't been any cars parked on the concrete. All the Mums had known each other and whoever was out kept an eye on any little one who was around. It had been friendly. Even when Colin was bigger and she didn't need to watch him she'd been able to hear him playing with his pals. She'd hear them shout when a goal was scored or they played soldiers. They hadn't had the bright coloured bikes the youngsters had now but they'd enjoyed being out there. Colin had never been short of pals.

She wiped down the table. She'd noticed the boys out yesterday. They had been on their bikes. She'd noticed the bikes with the red or blue coloured wheels. They seemed to do all sorts of tricks with them.

She'd remembered Colin as she watched them. The two boys had built a ramp with some wood and they were laughing and shouting. The dog was running with them and barking. She liked to hear the lads enjoying themselves out there. They never noticed her but she often watched them. She had left her gate open a lot last week with the weather being good. Their Mums didn't seem to meet at the back like they used to. Most of them had jobs and weren't around during the day but the boys were happy and they didn't seem any different from her boy when he'd first wobbled around the cobbles on his first grown-up bike.

They'd been sitting on the grass under the big tree one day and she'd been tempted to talk to them. She wouldn't have minded a close look at one of those bikes but she hadn't gone out. She'd been a bit frightened that they'd just think she was a silly old woman. Her two grandsons probably had bikes like that. She hadn't noticed when she'd last seen them. She didn't really see them often enough to keep up with what they were doing and what they were interested in.

Colin had phoned at the weekend. It had been the same thing he'd been saying. The house was too big for her to manage. She was too far away and there was nothing to keep her there any more.

She sighed. He didn't seem to know how much she liked the place. He'd grown up there but he never seemed to know that she just had to look around the house or the little bit of garden and it all came back to her. It had been her whole life and she liked to look around and remember what they'd done. He didn't know that she still watched the children outside, the little ones and the older lads and she could so easily slip back to when she was younger and her two were out there.

He was probably right when she thought about it. The house was bigger than she needed. She wasn't really able to afford a big bill though the house was in good condition. Sam had seen to that when he'd been alive and she kept some money set aside just in case the winter did any damage to the roof or the brickwork.

She knew that Colin wanted her to decide fairly soon. He'd managed to find a little place near him. He'd said she could bring a few bits and pieces of furniture and there'd be somebody to keep an eye on her if she ever got ill. Some sort of warden would check that she was fine. She sighed. She didn't like the idea. The kitchen dresser couldn't be moved down to some little room and anyway, it wouldn't be the same. It belonged in this kitchen.

She walked out into the yard. There was only one boy out on the grass. He was the youngest of the three who usually played out there. She smiled at him and he grinned.

'You're on your own today,' she said.

He nodded. 'The others are at school,' he said.

'My school is on holiday. It's a real waste of time when there's no one else around.'

She asked him if he'd like a biscuit and maybe a drink. She had some orange juice in the cupboard.

He came into the yard and talked to her about her plants. They chatted and he said he'd cut back her climbing plants if she told him what to do. He

was a nice lad. He did the plants and she told him about her children. He was interested in the tape she'd got from Elizabeth. He said he had a machine which would play it. He drank his juice and said he would go and get his machine.

She wasn't sure, but he said his Mum wouldn't mind. She said that if he was sure, she'd be careful with it. They made a deal. He said that she could borrow it and listen to – he said it carefully – *Liz's tape* and he'd pick up the machine in a couple of days. He'd said she could have it again if she got another tape. She'd said that she would tell his Mum and he assured her that there wouldn't be a problem. He was very kind. He'd shown her his bike. It was very different from the bike that Sam had got for Colin. The wheels were a sort of plastic material and it was brightly coloured with thick tyres. He'd told her all about it.

He went off to fetch his machine and she sat down again at the kitchen table. She hadn't done any weeding but there would be time to do it later.

The boy had said that he and his pals would give her a hand if she got stuck with the high bits. She looked at the plant which had reached the top of the wall. If one of them tidied all of it up, it would be fine all through the summer.

She'd have to tell Colin on the phone. She had decided and he would have to be told. She smiled.

Doing Well

'Moving anywhere would be better than living in this dump.' Sue banged her cup down on the kitchen table. 'I think Dad should jump at the chance of a move and just stop talking about it all the time. I'm sick of it.'

'Don't be an idiot,' Jill said. 'You don't just up and move without working it all out first. They have to talk about it. There's a lot more involved in it than you think.'

Sue pulled a face. 'I suppose you know all about it. I expect they've told you. You being so grown-up.'

Jill shook her head. 'I don't know any more about what Mum and Dad think about it than you do. What I do know is that you don't decide on moving just like that. I know there are loads of things they've got to think about – whether it would be good for everybody if we all had to move – they're even thinking about you.'

'I'm not in the least bit bothered,' Sue shrugged. 'I expect Bolton would be just like here when we did move. You'd get to go upstairs to study and I'd end up with the washing-up.'

'I do my share,' Jill said.

Sue shrugged again. 'Sometimes,' she muttered. They both looked out of the window.

'They cut the grass last week,' Sue said. 'They left it lying in heaps and the little kids had great fun throwing it around. I was watching them from our yard. You should have seen them.'

'Did you fancy joining in?' Jill smiled.

'What do you think I am?' Sue said. 'They were just toddlers. The two boys from our school piled it up again when the kids had finished.'

'D'you know them?' Jill asked.

'Not that well,' she said. 'I've seen them around at lunch time . . . they sometimes hang around together. They're not in my House . . . they often get the bus in the morning.'

'They're always out there with the dog,' Jill said.

'Must be really boring,' Sue sighed.

'You're always bored,' Jill said.

'You hardly lead a wild life either,' Sue snapped.

'I've got work to do,' Jill said, 'but I don't go around making everybody else fed up about it.'

'You're so perfect aren't you,' her sister said. Jill didn't bother to answer.

'Anyway,' Sue said, 'if we are moving it wouldn't be till after your exams so it wouldn't make any difference to you at all.'

'But I thought you weren't bothered?' Jill said. 'You've just said that you couldn't care less whether. . . .'

'I'm not bothered, not in the least,' Sue interrupted. 'I just wish they'd get on with it, that's all.' She put her cup down and walked out of the back door, slamming it behind her.

She almost bumped into old Mrs Baxter who was looking for her key in her shopping basket.

'Hello, love,' the old woman smiled. 'That walk from the shop always seems longer with a full basket.' She put the basket on the ground for a moment. Sue picked it up. 'I'll carry this in for you,' she said. 'I haven't seen you for ages.' She had often gone to the shop for the old lady when the weather had been bad.

Mrs Baxter looked at her. 'I'll make a pot of tea.'

Sue shook her head. 'No thanks, but I'll come in for a moment. I don't want to go back home just yet.'

Mrs Baxter nodded. 'You sit yourself down. I'll make myself a cup. You can have a biscuit if you're not watching your figure.' Sue thanked her.

'I was a bit stuck,' she said as the old woman poured the tea. 'I was having a row with our Jill and I came out but then I didn't have anywhere to go. You can't just hang around out here.'

'The boys seem to do that for hours,' Mrs Baxter said. 'Don't you get on with them . . . they're nice lads . . . I know the youngest one quite well now.'

Sue shrugged. 'It's different for them. They can still play around. Dad used to chase me out to play when I was younger but now if I even say I'm going into town, he nags about girls who hang around the streets and he makes a big thing of it . . . though it would likely be different if it was Jill. She swans off with her mates and then it's okay. They're all having a break from their work and it's good for them. I'm sick of it.'

Mrs Baxter didn't say anything.

Sue went on, 'And there's all this talk that we could be moving and I bet all they're worried about is her and her precious exams. I hope she fails the lot. That would teach her.'

'You wouldn't want that,' the old woman said quietly, 'and I'm sure that's not all they're thinking about. I nearly moved and I know what it's like . . . they'll be thinking about you too.'

'No bother about me,' Sue said. 'I'm the thick one so they can plonk me anywhere. It's not going to affect me is it? Anyway, one place is the same as another. I'd be just as stuck for things to do in Bolton and they'd treat me like a kid just like they do here. I wouldn't need to go out 'cause I wouldn't know anybody so that would be one less problem.' She sighed.

'What do you like about here?' Mrs Baxter asked. 'I found it was good to get my mind clear about things like that.'

Sue thought for a bit.

'What about your school?' Mrs Baxter asked.

'I'm not brainy like Jill,' she said.

'You like school and you don't do badly,' Mrs Baxter said. 'Your Mum told me all about your pictures and how pleased your teachers were.'

Sue looked surprised. 'School's okay really,' she said. 'We're doing work with fabric this year and there's a pottery teacher who says I can do some extra work for the Craft Centre in town. He said there's a sort of group I might be able to join. He said he could fix it . . . and this year when the play is on I'm going to be doing some of the scenery . . . it'll be great . . . that's if we're still here.'

'You'd miss all that,' the old woman said.

'It's not important like Jill's exams. I mean, they're hardly going to creep around to let me go into the front room to draw. I'm no good at the sort of things that matter to them.'

The old lady didn't say anything for a while.

'I think they'd take it seriously if they thought it mattered to you. They'd want to help you with your talent.'

'It's not talent with me,' Sue said. 'It's just something I'm not bad at. It's nothing special.'

'Special enough for them to think long and hard,' Mrs Baxter said. 'I mean, they're thinking hard from what you say, and Jill's exams wouldn't be affected. She'll likely be away at college soon so there's just going to be you at home for them to think about.'

Sue looked down at the table. 'It'll be funny without our Jill when she does go to college.'

'If she passes,' Mrs Baxter said.

'Oh she'll pass,' Sue said. 'She's good, you know, you should see her books. They're really hard and she's always working. They'd be stupid not to pass her. It would be awful. She worries about it too which is stupid 'cause she's always been clever but she's edgy at the moment . . . exam nerves, Mum calls it.'

The old woman was smiling at her.

Sue shrugged. 'I was in a bad mood when I said that about her failing. I'm just so fed up. I wish it were the same as it was before all this Bolton talk.'

'Have you told your Mum?' Mrs Baxter said.

Sue shook her head. 'They'd probably say there would be a Craft Group there though I'd probably not get in . . . even if there was one. It would all sound stupid to be making such a fuss about it.'

There was a knock at the door. Sue's Mum came in.

'I was hoping I'd find you here,' she said. She smiled at Mrs Baxter and told her that she had the knitting patterns she'd been looking for. Mrs Baxter nodded.

'Maybe you could pop in later and I could see you about wool,' she said. Sue's Mum looked surprised then agreed.

'Come on Sue,' she said. 'We've just had a phone call from one of your teachers. He's got you a place on a special course. He seems to think you're really something.'

'What did you say?' Sue said.

'We said we knew you were,' she laughed. 'Come and explain it all to your Dad. He thinks you're going to be carried off by a load of painters so you'd better tell him about it.'

Day Off

No one had expected the snow. Although it was almost November and it had been cold and windy, it was still a surprise to wake up and find that everything outside was white and it was sort of quiet. Rob had almost overslept. He was usually wakened by the milkman – either his whistling or the clink of the bottles on the doorstep. If that didn't work, the paper-boy's footsteps or the noise of the gate-catch did the trick. The snow had changed everything. All the morning sounds were muffled and Rob's Dad had come in to remind him of the time. Rob had stood at his window and stared out at the snow. He'd always been excited by the snow when he'd been little and, even now, it made the prospect of the journey to school something to look forward to.

He dressed quickly and kept an eye on the window in case Daniel was out early because of the snow. His Mum fussed more than usual and said that he wasn't leaving the house until he had a hot breakfast inside him. Skip was scratching at the door waiting for his morning walk out the back. Mum said she hoped Skip wouldn't get too wet as she knew the sort of state the kitchen floor would get into with this weather.

'Is my sledge here?' Rob asked as he bolted down his scrambled eggs.

'It didn't get left at the old place did it?' he asked. His Mum shook her head.

'It's in the big cupboard next to the washing machine but you're not touching it before you go to school or you'll never get there,' she said. 'According to the weather forecast, there's going to be more snow later this morning so it'll probably still be here when you get back.'

Rob picked up his parka and opened the back door. Skip shot out, then skidded to a halt. He stood perfectly still, seemed to balance on his toes and sniffed the snow. He lifted his front paw, licked it and then pushed his nose into the snow and snorted. Rob laughed at the look of surprise on the dog's face. Skip looked up at him and then leapt off through the snow, running and then stopping and having another sniff at the strange stuff which melted when he licked it. Rob stayed out with him as long as he could before taking the dog inside, rubbing him with his old towel and settling him in the kitchen. Skip looked disappointed. Rob grabbed his bag and met Daniel in the yard.

'Has to be a Friday doesn't it,' said Daniel. 'If it had just waited one day, it would have been perfect.'

Rob nodded. 'D'you have a sledge?' he asked.

'It's behind some junk in the outhouse,' said

Daniel, 'but I'll dig it out when we get in.'

'We could take Skip up the hill,' Rob said.

'Be safer if we go the back way,' Daniel nodded. 'There's a fair slope and no trees on that side.'

Nearer the school, there were a few snowballs flying around and kids were laughing and shouting more than usual. Daniel nudged Rob as a boy their age came towards them heading away from the school.

'Looks like Billy isn't going to be in today,' Daniel said. Rob smiled.

'No loss,' he said.

The boy stood in front of them. 'Will you tell Smithy that I've to go to the dentist,' he said to

Rob. He was grinning broadly. He was wearing jeans and an army sweater.

'Why don't you tell him yourself,' Rob said. 'You can catch him in the staffroom now and he'll give you a slip when he sees your appointment card.'

Billy grinned again. 'Lost me card haven't I, so if you tell him you met me on my way there.'

'Lost your uniform?' Daniel said.

'It's being washed,' Billy said. 'Me note is probably with the card I lost . . . this weather seems to have gone for my memory.'

He was holding an orange plastic sack. 'Anyway, if Smithy asks, you can tell him you met me on the way to the dentist, okay?' he said.

'With your plastic bag?' Daniel said.

'Please yourself,' Billy said. 'I'd probably have come in if it hadn't snowed but it's daft to waste it isn't it?'

'Pity about your dental appointment then,' Rob said. 'Gonna show your sledge to the dentist?'

Billy held up the plastic sack. 'This is just to pick up litter. There's a load of it up the Brinkburn Road.' With a wave, he walked off.

'He's going to get done, he is,' Daniel said. 'If somebody from the school drives along Brinkburn Road, they're surely not going to miss Billy flying down that hill on his sack.'

'If this keeps up, we'll likely not see much of him this term,' Rob said.

'No change, that,' Daniel said. 'Last term the sun took him to the park. The attendance woman picked him up fishing, didn't she?' Rob nodded. They laughed then split up to go to their form rooms.

Mr Smith was checking the register in Rob's classroom. He called Billy's name and looked up. The usual silence.

'Anyone know where Billy is?' he asked.

There were some laughs. John Brand said, 'He said something last night about the dentist, Sir.'

There were sniggers from the back.

'That boy's teeth must be a sight worth seeing . . . the hours of work that have been put into them.' Mr Smith marked his register.

Julie Scott shouted out, 'He was around this morning so he might just be late.' She looked over at Rob. 'Wasn't he talking to you outside school?' Rob mumbled but kept out of it. He didn't want to be involved with Billy. Another boy spoke. 'He had one of these sledge bags. There were a couple of first-years with him.'

Mr Smith nodded. He seemed tired of the subject. The bell rang and he took his class to Assembly.

The Head look worried. He said there was a problem. There had been a burst pipe or something and there was something wrong with one of the boilers as well. There was no water in the school. Everyone listened. He told them that the toilets would not be working. There were a few giggles but they stopped when he said they'd have to close but with luck it would be put right over the weekend. Most of the school seemed to be glancing out of the big windows. There was some snow falling and it looked inviting. The Head gave out details about letters to parents and lunches but Rob didn't really listen to anything else. If they hurried, he and Daniel could be back home in half an hour, be changed and have Skip up the hill in no time. He smiled to himself. Billy should have come in. He'd have got his mark and still been able to sledge. It was fairly noisy as they all left the hall.

Rob waited in the playground until Daniel came round from the other entrance. They decided to walk rather than wait for the bus.

'You can have some lunch at my place,' Rob said. 'We've got the whole day.'

Daniel nodded. 'Poor old Richard,' he said. 'He'll be sick. We could build a snowman outside his yard.' They walked quickly.

'Fancy that hill behind the park,' Daniel said, 'since we've got the time?'

'Bit steep,' Rob said, 'and not great for Skip. We'll stick to our own patch. It'll be okay.' They were running by the time they reached the cobbled back lane. Daniel ran in front and went in to his house to change. Rob met his Mum in the hall and told her what had happened.

'You've got the luck of the devil you have,' she said. She smiled all the same.

Skip barked. He seemed to know it was all a treat. Rob didn't waste time. He and Skip were back in the yard in minutes. Daniel joined them. They took the path to the hill.

Daniel had a plastic sledge and Rob pulled a strong wooden one his uncle had made. Skip wasn't sure what to make of the things. He chased them as the boys pulled them over the snow.

They reached the bottom of the path to the hill and stopped. From there, they could see the grassy slope which went along the side of Brinkburn Road. Rob stopped.

'We'll probably see an orange flash going at great speed. Billy was going to try out his plastic sack down there,' he said.

'He's daft,' Daniel said. 'It's too near the road. He'll be spotted dead easily.'

'Nobody will notice now we're closed. He managed to get a couple of first-years to go with him,' Rob said.

'Idiots,' said Daniel. 'They'll end up in bother if they go around with him. If their Year Head twigs, they'll be watched.'

They heard the police car. Then they saw the blue flashing lights. Rob reeled in Skip's lead and without talking about it, they both moved towards the road at the bottom of the slope. By the end of the path they were running. They didn't know why. Skip ran with them. They reached the dual carriageway at the end of the grass.

One police car was stopped at an angle. Another car was stopped. The driver was out of the car. There was a policeman with him. The man was talking, and half crying. Rob and Daniel stopped and stared. Billy was there. He had his orange sack. It was on the road, near him. He had a cut on his head and he was holding his arm near to him. An

ambulance man was talking to him. Billy didn't
seem to know what was going on. He was staring at
the road. A few yards in front of the car, there was a
boy lying on the road and his arms were wrong.
They weren't in the right position. Another man
brought a blanket from the ambulance and put it
over the boy. He put the blanket right over him.
There was only blood on the road to see. He was all
covered up. Billy started to be sick. Rob pulled
Daniel's arm and they turned away.

They walked back home. They didn't speak all
the way. Daniel was very white. They didn't bother

about the path up to the hill. They left the sledges in Daniel's yard. Skip didn't pull on his lead. They stopped at the trees on the grass. Rob spoke first.

'They must have been going down hill on the sack . . . together,' he said.

'Right on to the road,' said Daniel.

'They didn't stand a chance,' Rob said, 'not with the traffic on that road . . . that young kid . . . he should have known.'

'Billy seemed to be okay,' Daniel said, 'I don't think he was really badly hurt.'

'So much for his good idea,' Rob said. 'He'll be in real bother this time . . .'

The Bonny (1)

'This place is getting really scruffy,' Rob said.

Daniel and Richard nodded. Rob passed his crisp bag around and the three of them looked at the grass. There were deep tyre marks on the grass near the concrete, pools of oil and broken glass and beer cans over on the cobbles near the end house. Rob's Dad had been sweeping more glass from just

outside their yard. He stopped next to the boys.

'The folk from the end are turning this place into a tip,' Rob said. 'It's not fair.'

His Dad sat down on the wall. 'It's a shame,' he said. 'When I was your age, this place was always kept tidy. It would have been a real crime for anyone to mess up The Bonny.'

'It was tidy right up till last month,' Daniel said, 'until the blokes from the end started fixing and testing their cars on it.'

'And dumping their bottles and cans,' Richard added, 'and leaving all sorts of rubbish on the grass.'

'Can't you do something about it, Dad?' said Rob.

'I don't know,' his Dad frowned. 'We haven't been here that long, Rob, and I don't want to start making trouble. Your mother wouldn't be too pleased if I started playing war with folk who live around here.'

'But you lived around here when you were little so that must count for something,' Rob said.

His Dad shrugged. 'I don't know if there's a lot we can do,' he said. 'Maybe if we put a bit of effort into the bonfire this year, folk might take some interest in the place and see that it's a good spot for the kids. I don't know.' He walked back to the house. The boys stayed on the wall, looking out at the grass.

'I think we should ask your Mum,' Daniel said to Richard.

'Why?' Richard looked surprised.

'Well, she might know what we could do,' Daniel said. 'I mean she's good at getting her own way isn't she. When we went to the hospital with Rob that time, she was straight up to the desk and we didn't have to wait.'

'You mean pushy,' Rob said. He was smiling but he felt a bit let down that his Dad hadn't been able to help and Daniel seemed sure that Richard's Mum would.

Daniel shook his head. 'I just think she might have some ideas,' he said. 'I mean it wouldn't be fighting if it was his Mum. She can sound really official but can do it, sort of friendly so that nobody would be annoyed. They might think your Dad wanted a scrap.'

Rob seemed happier when it was put like that. 'We could give it a try,' he said. 'Is she in?' Richard nodded so the three of them headed for his house. Richard told his Mum they wanted to talk to her so she made a cup of coffee, poured lemonade for them and they sat down at the kitchen table.

Daniel described the mess and the state that the grass at the back was getting into. 'It's not just that it looks awful,' he said, 'last week all the little kids from the Home got oil all over their clothes, Skip's had his paw cut with the glass and when they start driving the cars over the grass, they churn it all up and it's not even safe to play. It's worse for the little ones. I know we can't say the land belongs to us but they've spoiled it and it's just not fair. One of the lads who hangs around there broke some of the branches last week. They're going to wreck the place and it can be great when it's tidy. Kids have played on The Bonny since Rob's Dad was our age.'

'I know,' she said. 'I had to sweep the glass away before I took the car out yesterday . . . but what do you want me to do?'

'We thought you'd know how to get them stopped,' Daniel said, ''cause you could tell them in a sort of grown-up way and they might take notice and not take a swing at you . . . if you know what I mean.'

She smiled at them. 'I think you've got the right idea but I'm sure if you go about it the right way, you might be able to manage it by yourselves.'

'What can we do?' Richard said.

His Mum sipped her coffee. 'You could find out what other people think, by asking properly and then you could talk to the community policeman or someone like that and tell him what you've just told me and then when you've got some backing you could help tidy the place up.'

'Rob's Dad said if this year's bonfire was decent, folk might see that it's not a bad patch,' Daniel said.

'That's right,' she said, 'and if you can find enough people on your side, maybe you can get them to take an interest in the land. I'm sure the people who have young children want it to be clean and fairly safe but you're going to have to organize it. I'll be happy to help out once you've got some support. Maybe if people meet and have a coffee you might get some help in keeping your patch the way everyone wants it. It's worth a try . . . it's only about four weeks till the Bonfire.'

'I don't know if we can bring in the police,' said Rob. It sounded a bit drastic to him.

'You can go and talk,' she said. 'I'm pretty sure they'd listen to you . . . but I think you have to get your facts together and find out what people think.'

The boys didn't play much for the next three days. They spoke to the lady who was on duty at the Home; they spoke to Mrs Baxter and her neighbours on both sides. When they saw the Dad of the girls from their school he sent them to another house and after they'd been there, the woman told them to see someone she'd been speaking to.

Everyone seemed to feel that they were right and people were pleased to get a chance to talk about the complaints.

They made a list and kept a note of all the complaints. Richard's Mum gave them the number to telephone and they were given a time to go and talk to the policeman.

The night before the meeting, they were standing on the cobbles with Skip when one of the lads from the end house roared up in a car he'd been working on. Skip barked as the car drove quickly past him. The lad drove backwards on to the grass, revving the engine. It's tyres churned up the grass, leaving it bare and muddy.

Daniel decided to speak. He stepped forward. 'We're finding out if the people who live around here are keen to tidy up the place 'cause it's getting scruffy and it's a shame because all the little kids play out here and it can be okay when it's kept in good nick.'

'So what,' the lad said.

'Well, you're making a mess of the grass with that kind of driving,' Rob said.

'Look son,' the lad said, 'is it your grass?'

Rob shook his head.

'Well don't try to tell me what to do with it,' he said.

'But there's oil and glass and bits of car, not to mention the cans and the rubbish,' Richard said.

The lad turned to him. 'You just shut your face unless you want it shut for you. This is junk land and we can please ourselves what we do on it so don't think that me and my mates are going to bother with a bunch of kids behaving like old women about some bit of grass.'

'It's not just us . . .' Daniel started.

'Just get lost huh,' the lad said and walked off. He threw his empty cigarette box on to the ground as he walked.

'It's not going to be easy,' Richard said.

They were a bit nervous about their meeting at the police station but nobody treated them as if they were being stupid. The community policeman took all the details, checked the big map and listened to what they had to say.

'Well,' he said, 'it's public land but some of it is official car parking space and any cars parked there would have to have tax and insurance and everything. The council wouldn't be too keen on the grass area being damaged. They wouldn't want anyone to run a business on their land either . . . doubt if the landlord of the flats would be happy about his tenants turning the place into a garage or scrap-yard. I think you can leave this with us now.'

'How do we stand as far as our bonfire is concerned?' Richard said. 'I mean that grass area has always been called The Bonny 'cause that's where the kids have the bonfire . . . what I was wondering is . . . if we say they can't mess the place up with cars and rubbish, can we still build our bonfire?'

The policeman smiled. 'I don't think there are any plans to stop all bonfires this year . . . and I'm sure you three aren't going to cause damage since you've taken the trouble to come here and get everyone interested in keeping the place decent.'

He shook hands with them when they left.

'We'll see what happens now,' Rob said, 'but we'll have to keep at it . . . some of the folk we talked to said they wanted to meet and talk to the other folk who live around The Bonny.'

'My Mum said she'd help if we got it started but we can let them get on with the meetings and we'll stick to keeping it looking okay,' Richard said. 'I don't really fancy sitting round with the coffee and sandwiches while they all natter.'

Daniel laughed. 'Hope they don't get too carried away,' he said.

'I can just see The Bonny with picnic tables and umbrellas and everything and no space for the bonfire.'

'We could walk around with those sticks with the spikes on the end and pick up the litter,' Rob joined in.

'Come on then,' Richard said. 'We could make a start with a bin bag and get the cans picked up . . . it'll be an improvement.'

On the Wall

'Fancy swimming tomorrow?' Rob said.

They were sitting on the low wall outside Richard's house.

'I have to go into town with my Mum sometime,' Richard said. 'I need trainers and she said she'd look at the jackets in Cordon's. I don't know when she's going in but if it's morning, I'll be okay for the afternoon.'

'I'm going to my Dad's,' Daniel said. 'I might not be back till Sunday.' Rob groaned. Daniel looked uncomfortable. 'It's okay though, at Dad's,' Daniel said. 'I can go swimming there if I want to . . . there's a decent pool. We've used it quite a lot. It doesn't have a wave machine like in town but you can have a good swim.'

'Great,' said Rob, 'but we're here when you're there.'

Daniel shrugged.

'He has to see his Dad,' Richard said. 'I mean, these things are sort of worked out aren't they and you're supposed to stick to them . . . it's only fair.'

'I know,' Rob said. 'I'm not saying it's any-body's fault. It's just a pity that it's at the weekend that's all.'

'It's not every weekend,' Richard said. 'Sometimes it's a Friday and during the holidays it's often during the week.'

'Hey,' said Daniel, 'I'm still here you know . . . I can talk for myself. I like going to my Dad's if you must know. It's just now and again . . . I'd quite like to stop here. But I don't like to change it too often . . . it's like Richard says.'

'It's funny though isn't it,' Rob said. 'I mean my Dad's always keen enough to go to the match and I go fishing with him and my Uncle Alex, but it's not like a regular thing . . . and I never just hang around with him for a full day. He'd wonder what was up.'

'But he's at home all the time,' Daniel said. 'He's around in the morning and every night so you don't have to see him in one lump do you?'

'Mind you,' Rob said, with a grin, 'when my Dad has a lot of overtime, you probably see more of yours in a weekend than I see of mine in a month . . . if you counted it all up that is.'

'With the hours my Dad works, there are times I hardly see him at all,' Richard said.

Nobody spoke for a while

'Parents are funny aren't they?' Richard said. 'I never thought about it when I was little.' He picked at some loose stones.

'I still don't,' Rob said, 'so it's probably just you. You think about things you do.'

Skip pushed his nose against Rob's ankle. 'I suppose it's just the same as me with him,' Rob said nodding at Skip. 'I mean it's up to me to look after him and even when it means a bit of work, like on a wet, miserable morning, it still has to be done. Parents are probably like that. There are probably times when they're not dead interested but they have to be, so . . . they just get on with it I would think.'

'They must be interested,' Richard said, 'or they wouldn't have had us in the first place.'

'I don't mean they're not interested ever,' Rob said. 'I mean, I don't think anyone can be dead keen all the time. Anyway, loads of folk even have kids they didn't mean to have and some just don't bother. Curly from the Home had a Mum and Dad but they just gave up with him after a while.'

'My Mum only gets sick of me when the place is in a mess and my stuff's all over. But she's never really serious about it . . . not serious enough to be really mad. She just yells a bit and goes on but it's not like a huge row . . . just a nag,' Daniel said. 'It would be different if I was in real bother like some kids are. She would go mad . . . so would my Dad,' he added.

Rob nodded. 'Jason Wright's Dad once came to our house and said I'd pinched a couple of pounds from their house and my Dad nearly had a fit. I said I didn't, but Mum had to stop him getting a hold of me. Then Mr Wright came back about eleven o'clock at night and said that Jason had taken the money and tried to shove the blame on to me 'cause I'd been round at his house. Dad got me out of bed to tell me. I think he felt a bit funny about it,' Rob smiled, 'but I think if he'd got a hold of me when Jason's Dad said I'd done it, he'd have given me a good hiding.'

Daniel shrugged, 'Curly's Dad gave him a few good hidings and Billy Wilkin's Dad used to nearly cripple him but it made no difference . . . Curly still pinches and Billy's a rogue. Even that kid getting killed after going with Billy hasn't made a lot of difference. Billy's still nickin' off school and he'll lie through his teeth to get out of bother. He doesn't care.'

'I think when I have a kid I'll be quite hard,' Rob said, 'but I'd like to have some fun with him as well and let him have a dog and go places with him and that sort of thing.'

'When they're little . . . that's when you're strict and there's no messing,' Daniel nodded, 'and then when they get bigger, you can talk to them about things and explain what it's like and you get more friendly 'cause the kid can understand more and can maybe see why you've been strict.'

Rob and Daniel nodded.

Richard frowned. 'I think my Mum . . . well, she doesn't really work like that.'

'She treats you as if you're grown-up doesn't she?' Rob said.

'No she doesn't,' Richard interrupted. 'She wasn't keen on our camp.'

'No, but she asks you proper questions about things and she wants to know what you think. She took us all really seriously when we were annoyed about the state this place was in and she's always listening to what you say,' Rob said.

'Even if we know it's rubbish,' Daniel said.

Richard looked embarrassed, 'She's okay,' he said. 'She's never done stupid things like showing you up at school when we had the play. Peter Harper's mother had on a really stupid hat and she kept clapping loudly when Peter was on and she was kissing and hugging him and being really loud with him. He felt a real fool. She wouldn't do that. Every time somebody has a row with Peter, his mother is mentioned and they blow kisses at him. He's really sick.'

'Mothers like to grab kids,' Rob said. He sort of smiled.

'Yeah,' Daniel said, 'but at our age they're not sort of open about it are they?'

Richard looked at them both. Rob grinned and picked at some pebbles from the wall. Daniel pulled at a loose thread on his jeans.

'Is it like that with you two . . . even yet?' Richard said. He made his question sound casual.

Rob laughed again. 'I suppose so,' he said. 'It's like you said, they don't do it in the middle of the shops but, you know, it's different at home, isn't it? You're not bothered about at home . . . that's different.'

'I've really got two homes,' Daniel said. 'I feel okay at Dad's too. Even though it's here where I have most of my stuff, I have my room at Dad's and it's just mine and we cook daft meals and some weeks, we end up talking really late.'

'Sounds okay,' Rob said. He felt a bit guilty about going on at Daniel.

'I never do anything like that with my Dad,' Richard said.

Daniel seemed pleased.

'Be even nicer if he lived at the end of the street,' Rob said, 'then it would be fine for all of us.'

Skip pulled at the toe of Rob's trainer and did his pretend growl.

'He's getting fed up,' Rob said, 'he's about ready for a meal.' Rob stood up and Skip danced around him, looking pleased.

A car bumped over the cobbles. Daniel stood up. 'It's my Dad,' he said. 'He must be picking me up tonight.'

The car stopped next to them. His Dad wound down the window. 'There's a festival day or something on at the pool tomorrow. I thought it might be good if you asked your pals to come. If you let me

know I can fix it with your Mum,' his Dad said.

Daniel looked at Rob and Richard.

'It'll be great,' he said. 'Last year all the stuff was laid on, food and everything.'

'Sounds good,' Rob said.

'Would be great,' Richard added.

The car moved on up to Daniel's house.

'That's another thing about parents,' Rob said. 'They often do something that's really right . . . and you don't know how.'

Skip barked. He'd waited long enough.

The Bonny (2)

Rob jumped out of bed almost as soon as he woke. It was still dark but he pulled back his curtains and peered outside. He held his breath. It seemed to have stopped raining. He pulled on his clothes and raced downstairs. Skip bounded behind him. He seemed to think that an early morning walk was likely. He followed Rob out into the back yard. Rob opened the gate and went outside. It wasn't really light enough to see much. Rob shivered slightly, ran his hand over the grass and checked that there was still a dark outline in the middle of the grassy triangle. He shivered again and headed back inside. Skip looked disappointed but since he still hadn't had his breakfast, he followed quite happily.

Rob's Dad met them in the kitchen.

'Do you two know it's Sunday?' he said. 'You're never this lively on a school day.'

'It's not raining Dad,' Rob said.

His Dad grinned. 'The weather forecast said it would be fine . . . and you did check about four times yesterday so you can't be that surprised.'

Rob sat at the table. His Dad made tea and some toast. Skip munched his biscuits. 'It would have been awful if it had been a school day,' Rob said, 'or pouring.'

'Maybe next year they'll change the date for you so that it falls at the weekend again. Or you could have Guy Fawkes night in July for a change, to have a better chance with the weather.' He handed Rob a mug of tea.

'D'you think the wood will be dry enough?' Rob asked.

'Should be okay,' his Dad said. 'That plastic sheeting that Daniel's Dad got for you will have helped. We'll get it going.'

'Place looks good doesn't it?' Rob got up and walked over towards the window.

His Dad laughed. 'If you three had got your way that grass out there would look like a bowling green. You've checked every blade of it.'

Rob sat down again. 'At least the folk at the end have given up spoiling the place since the people from the Council came around. They've been quite careful where they park their cars.'

'They've had you and everybody you roped in glaring at them for the last few weeks,' his Dad grinned. 'I think even the birds are a bit nervous about sitting on the trees.'

Rob took another slice of toast. 'Folk have been great,' he said. 'The place looks a lot better. That's why it would be awful if it had rained . . . though we still can't be sure that anybody will be interested in the bonfire. At least if it's a fine night, it might be tempting. Jill and Sue's Dad said he might bring out a sort of barbecue thing if it was a decent night.' He frowned and looked again at the window.

There was a knock at the back door. Skip didn't bark. Rob's Dad shook his head. 'It's the other two,' he said. 'I'm going back to bed for an hour. You three can sit here and worry about wet fireworks.'

Rob poured two more mugs of tea.

'I didn't bother much about Bonfire Night last year,' Richard said. 'There was a display in the park but it was nothing special. You had to stand around for a while.'

'We had one here,' Daniel said, 'but it wasn't all that good. It was mainly for the little kids. The folk from the Home did most of the work, but it was just sparklers for the little ones and a few rockets. The Guy was pretty useless.'

'We don't know that ours will be any better. Jill and Sue aren't bringing it out until we get started . . . it might be pathetic.' Rob looked worried. 'We can't even be sure that folk will be that interested. I mean, Bonfire Night's not like Christmas is it?'

Richard shrugged. 'We'll just have to wait and see. But the place looks better, and they needn't be interested in Guy Fawkes. It might feel just like a sort of party.'

Rob stroked Skip's head. 'I hope so,' he said. 'I

got Skip a bone from the butchers as his treat. He's staying in . . . at least till all the fireworks are over.'

Daniel looked at the clock. 'We could check the bonfire. We don't want any of it pinched . . . before tonight.'

'Today's going to really drag,' Rob said.

By seven, the plastic sheet had been taken off the pile of wood. The three boys checked and re-checked the boxes of fireworks.

First, a few people came out on to the grass. Then about a dozen children banged through the gate from the Home. Sparklers were handed out and lit. Rob's Dad lit the lanterns he'd set up on the yard walls. Mrs Baxter brought out a huge tray of sausage rolls and buns and set them out on the wooden table. The place suddenly seemed to be busy. Jill and Sue's Dad was wearing a striped apron and handing out sausages and baked potatoes in tinfoil.

Rob watched the people laughing. He felt funny. He wanted to yell and run about. There was a cheer. Jill and Sue were pushing a wheelbarrow with a Guy in it. It was about six feet tall with a suit

and a bowler hat. Sparklers fizzled from its pockets. It had huge ears and a wide grin. It was lifted on to the bonfire and then Richard's Dad lit the wood. There was another cheer as the flames shot up. Someone had set up a loudspeaker and the music started. Everyone seemed to be laughing and talking. Another rocket shot into the air and a shower of green, red and silver sparks lit up the sky.

Rob sat on the edge of the wall. He ate his hot potato and watched the people. Mrs Baxter was standing with the twins. She was laughing and had a bright red knitted hat pulled down over her ears. Rob grinned at her and she waved.

The little kids were racing around – yelling and running round the bonfire.

Rob laughed at them. He could feel how excited they were. It was going fine. He felt someone pull his sweater. Beth was warmly wrapped up and was almost hidden in her anorak with her hood up. He lifted her up on to the wall so that she could see the Catherine Wheel fireworks which had just been lit. She held on to his hand tightly. She didn't speak, she just stared at the fireworks and smiled. Rob couldn't stop watching her. He held her anorak. She felt very small and light. She giggled as a bunch of sparklers in the Guy's hat exploded. Her mother walked over to Rob.

'It's past this little girl's bedtime,' she said, 'but I suppose it's a bit special tonight isn't it?' He nodded.

Beth's mother lifted her from the wall and carried her towards their house.

Daniel and Richard ran up with cans of pop and a plate of sausages.

'Great isn't it?' Richard said. 'Everybody says so,' he added.

'There's loads more to eat,' Daniel said, 'and the man from the shop gave four trays of these drinks.' He emptied the can he was holding. They sat on the wall for a while, just watching.

'There'll be some clearing up job to do tomorrow,' Rob said.